MW00890036

Wisdom quote

Journals

Made in United States
Orlando, FL
18 November 2024

54059050R00074